My pregna

By Kendra Perley

For permissions contact:

thematernalcanvas@gmail.com

Table of Contents

To my husband, Mark, who has been my biggest supporter in everything I do. You are my best friend, a wonderful husband, and an amazing father. You make it all look so easy.

To our son, A., who inspires me every day. Thank you for your light and love. You made me a mom and for that I will be forever grateful.

And to our son, P., who is such a joy and full of love. You brought such warmth to our family.

To all the type 1 diabetic mothers who have endured the rocky road of pregnancy, including my mom, Deb, and sister, Nikki. You are stronger than you know.

Preface

This book grew out of the blog entries I wrote during my first pregnancy. As a first-time expectant mother, I was excited and nervous about what my pregnancy would be like. As a type 1 diabetic (T1D), I was on the hunt for as much information as I could find about what to expect. The problem was there really wasn't a lot out there about pregnant diabetic mothers, other than stories of what could go horribly wrong. Because of that, I decided I wanted to document what my experience was like, thinking at best it would relate to another mother in her journey, and at the very least it would be something I could look back upon years from now.

The purpose of this book is to provide insight into my experience during my first pregnancy as a type 1 diabetic. In my efforts to understand other T1D mothers' experiences, I have found comfort in knowing that we are not alone. Although every woman and every pregnancy is different, T1D is the common thread that weaves us together, and it is comforting to know that other women out there can relate to the roller coaster ride that is enduring a pregnancy with T1D.

That said, this book is my personal experience. It's an intimate glimpse into my thoughts, feelings, excitement, and worries during my pregnancy. I am not a medical professional, and do not offer any medical advice.

Chapter 1: All About Me

At the time of my first pregnancy, I was 27 years old and had been living with type 1 diabetes for 20 years. When I was diagnosed at the young age of seven, I did not fully grasp the magnitude of living with diabetes. Because my mom was a type 1 diabetic, I knew there would be finger pokes, insulin shots, and less sugary food – basically a kid's worst nightmare. At that point, I certainly didn't think about managing my diabetes through pregnancy later in life.

But while I learned to manage my illness, I never let it get in the way of what I wanted to do. I played a variety of sports growing up, had sleepovers with friends, lived the typical college experience, and found an incredibly loving and supportive partner to call my husband. So when it came time to plan a pregnancy, I knew I wouldn't let my diabetes control my life. Instead, I knew I had to control my diabetes.

I consider myself a reasonably responsible diabetic, and I credit that to being diagnosed with the disease so young. Although no one wants to see a child take on the responsibility of managing a serious lifelong illness, being so young when I was diagnosed allowed me to adapt to the diabetic lifestyle at an early age and follow it through to adulthood.

Don't get me wrong, I'm not a perfect diabetic. I've had ups and downs in the span of 20 years, and no one is perfect. I indulge now and again, but I always make sure to take the appropriate insulin. But every day is different, and sometimes my body decides to do its own thing despite my best efforts. Prior to and during my first pregnancy, I worked to maintain an active lifestyle, exercising three to four days a week. (Things have changed a bit since becoming a mom of two, and my regular workouts have unfortunately taken a backseat.)

Taking control of my health has allowed me to live 20 years as a diabetic with no complications, and for that I feel very blessed. I have used an insulin pump for nine years, and although there are days when I want to toss it out of the window, 99.9% of the time I love it and it makes managing my diabetes so much easier.

Growing up, I knew I wanted kids eventually, and although I knew that being diabetic while pregnant would be different, I didn't fully grasp the seriousness of it until I was older. My mom was T1D when she gave birth to me and my sister, so I knew having babies was possible, even though she experienced her own struggles and complications during pregnancy. It wasn't until I was older that I learned of the serious complications that can occur during pregnancy while being a T1D, including increased risk of miscarriage and stillbirth, as well as other complications that could affect both baby and mom.

When it came time for my husband and I to start thinking about children, I knew I needed to get my blood sugars under tight control. I did research and spoke with my endocrinologist about what I needed to do before I got pregnant to ensure a healthy pregnancy and baby, and her suggestion was to get my hemoglobin A1c (HbA1c) at 6.0% or below. I definitely saw this as doable as my HbA1c was running in the 7.0% or below range. So that was my goal and I was going to work hard to reach it.

The remainder of this book details my experience after learning of my first pregnancy. I truly hope there are women out there who can find a connection to my experience. There will be moments of humor, and moments that are more emotional. But this is the difficult, beautiful, and joyous experience of a pregnant type 1 diabetic.

Chapter 2: Zero to 18 Weeks in 60 Seconds

I found out I was pregnant on December 30, 2014. I hadn't been feeling quite right for a couple days. My period was due any day, but this definitely felt different from PMS. One of the first signs of pregnancy that I noticed was my blood sugars. They would linger in the 150-200 range even after giving the correct bolus for what I was eating and doing correction boluses when my blood sugar wouldn't come down. It wasn't until I completely changed my basal rates and insulin-to-carb ratios that my blood sugars returned to their "normal" levels.

I picked up a pregnancy test on the way home from work that night, and sure enough, two blue lines appeared almost instantly. I was very excited, but also a little nervous. I knew this meant I would be embarking upon a completely new adventure as a pregnant type 1 diabetic, and there could be serious risks.

I pushed those thoughts out of my head for the moment and tried to relish in the reality that my husband and I were going to have a baby. I sprung the happy news on my husband as soon as he walked in the door, and he was over-the-moon happy.

The realization that I was pregnant soon became abundantly clear as the first trimester symptoms kicked in. My emotions were a mess. I am not an overly emotional person, so the fact that I found myself weepy was one of my first symptoms.

Only a few days before I found out that we were expecting, I found myself lying in bed when all of a sudden, I was frantically concerned about whether two boxes of stuffed animals from my childhood, which we were storing at my in-laws' house, had been donated to Goodwill without my knowledge.

I don't find myself too attached to material objects, and I'm not overly sentimental, but I told my husband that it would break my heart to know that piece of my childhood was gone. I couldn't let it go. I told him that he immediately needed to email his mom and figure out if those two precious boxes were still in their possession.

I could barely sleep that night worrying about it. I cried and cried at the thought of possibly never seeing those useless items that were just taking up space. This behavior was out of the ordinary for me, and looking back, it was definitely my first indicator that I was preggo.

Along with my unsteady emotions, I was tired – more than I had ever been in my entire life. And when I say tired, I mean I could barely keep my eyelids pried open. At this point in time, I was participating in a strenuous exercise program six days a week, and I could hardly drag myself out of the house for a workout. My energy level at the gym had dropped dramatically. I was no longer excited for kickboxing, and I soon made the decision to tone down my exercise regimen.

Nausea was the next to kick in around week six. I feel lucky in the sense that I never had any vomiting, but there were times when my nausea was so bad that I could barely stand to breathe.

Along with nausea and extreme fatigue, I got food aversions and cravings early. I've always been a turkey and chicken kind of person, but during my first trimester, poultry did not sound good to me whatsoever. In fact, all meat made me want to gag.

I did have a few odd cravings. The first was SpaghettiOs, which I hadn’t eaten in years. I felt like a five-year-old, cracking open a can of pasta swimming in tomato sauce. But, man, was that canned pasta tasty.

The oddest craving I had was for a fiestada. For those not in the know, this is a small, pizza-like entree that was served for school lunches when I was a kid – something I hadn't eaten in probably 20 years. For whatever reason, that sounded amazing to me and I was able to find a homemade recipe online. I was excited to give it a try, and though it wasn't bad, it just wasn't the same.

Since the homemade attempt didn't satisfy my craving, I was convinced that we could find a fiestada somewhere. Bless my husband for remembering seeing such an item at one of our local grocers. As luck would have it, we were able to track it down. It was the exact same as I remember being served in my school cafeteria. It tasted exactly as I'd hoped, but one was enough, and I never had that craving again.

Along with the nausea and food aversions/cravings, I was plagued with oh-so-uncomfortable bloating. I could barely eat two bites without my stomach ballooning up like I was well into my third trimester. I found that one of the best ways to combat this was to eat five or six smaller meals a day. Not only did this help to eliminate some of the bloating, but I found that it also helped maintain my blood sugars at a steady level.

The first trimester was a tricky time of trying to figure out my insulin doses. This is a time when blood sugar levels dip, resulting in several occurrences of hypoglycemia. I would have several low blood sugars during the day, and at least one or two overnight. This was a little frustrating, but working with my endocrinologist and seeing her every three to four weeks got me to where my basal and bolus levels were keeping me from hitting such dramatic lows.

It was during this time that I decided to get a continuous glucose monitor (CGM), and I found it to be extremely beneficial in learning my blood sugar patterns. I saw my endocrinologist for the first time during my pregnancy when I was six weeks along; at that time, my HbA1c reading was 6.6%. I was happy with this, but I knew I could get it down a little more. Sure enough, at my 12-

week checkup, it was down to 5.7%. I was ecstatic. This was the lowest I could ever remember it being. To put it in perspective, a non-diabetic person's hemoglobin A1c levels should range between 4.0% and 5.6%.

I suspected that my OB/GYN might refer me to a specialist since I am T1D and considered "high risk" even though my blood sugars were well maintained, and sure enough, that's what she did. She referred me to a perinatologist (also known as a maternal fetal medicine doctor/MFM), and the two of them began tag-teaming my prenatal care.

I must say, getting referred to my perinatologist was one of the best experiences of my pregnancy. My doctor was knowledgeable about diabetes and the risks of pregnancy, and I felt completely comfortable in his care. One of the bonuses of seeing a perinatologist is having an ultrasound at each checkup. I got to see my little baby boy (we found out the gender at the 16-week ultrasound) about once a month, so I loved getting to watch him grow.

Being diabetic while pregnant means having a few more tests done than the average woman, and I was starting to feel like a lab rat. Along with the typical first trimester testing to screen the baby for chromosomal and other birth defects, I had the unfortunate task of doing a 24-hour urine sample, which is exactly what it sounds like. To check my kidney functions, I had to collect my urine for 24 hours in a jug and keep it in the refrigerator. I was grateful that I was working at home at that time.

I also had an EKG, which I never had before, to see if having diabetes had done any damage to my heart.

There was a lot of poking and prodding during my first trimester, but I reminded myself that it was to ensure a healthy baby and pregnancy. I was incredibly grateful for the medical team I had supporting me every step of the way.

Chapter 3: What's on the Menu?

Diet is always a topic of discussion during pregnancy. When "eating for two" and diabetic, diet is incredibly important to maintain your target blood sugars. The first trimester consisted of whatever I could bring myself to eat, and I will admit that a lot of what I was craving was not the healthiest. Once I was well into my second trimester, I found myself able to stomach some healthier choices.

I learned that eating six smaller meals not only helped with digestion and reduced bloating, but it also kept my blood sugar levels steadier throughout the day. Below is an example of what I ate on a daily basis.

Breakfast: I started just about every day with a cup or so of regular Cheerios and unsweetened vanilla almond milk. I don't care too much for cow's milk, which is why I used almond milk. Along with cereal, I had a serving of light Greek yogurt. If I was feeling especially hungry, I ate an apple or orange with that meal. I also like V8 Fusion Light juice, so some days I would substitute that for the fruit.

Morning Snack: A granola bar and some protein, such as cheese or peanut butter.

Lunch: Dinner leftovers! My other options were light frozen entrees, but I tried to only eat one or two of these a week because of the sodium content.

Afternoon Snack: I was usually craving fruit in the afternoon, so my favorite go-to snack was an apple with peanut butter or cheese. If I was feeling especially hungry, I added in some crackers or chips. I had to get my BBQ potato chip fix every now and again! Every so often, I was also in the mood for a piece or two of whole wheat toast with a little peanut butter.

Dinner: I cooked a homemade dinner at least six days a week, and this was probably my largest meal of the day. I made a multitude of recipes, but they were all typically chicken or turkey based: chicken tacos, grilled chicken breast, turkey meatloaf, BBQ chicken sandwiches, et cetera. Basically for this meal, I incorporated protein, carbs, and veggies.

Bedtime/Post-workout Snack: We typically got back from the gym around 8:00 pm, so it was then that I usually ate a little snack. I ate protein to keep my blood sugar steady, so I had another Greek yogurt or fruit with some peanut butter or cheese.

This is what an average day looked like for me when pregnant - pretty simple, nothing too exciting. I tried to mix things up for variety, such as the flavor of yogurt or fruit, and our dinnertime meals. Of course, there were exceptions to this meal plan. I would say we ate away from home no more than a handful of times a month, and there were occasions when I allowed myself a special treat such as ice cream. Everything in moderation.

One food that I made sure to stay away from was pizza. Like other diabetics, this is the absolute worst thing for me to eat. My blood sugar will be on track right after eating a couple slices, then it will skyrocket through the roof a few hours later and just decide to hang out up in space for a while. Since this is frustrating when I'm not pregnant, I knew I didn't want to deal with that stress while I was expecting, so I happily steered clear of the pizza train.

Overall, I was happy with my eating habits and how it affected my blood sugars and weight gain during pregnancy. Having a regular meal plan in place was beneficial.

Chapter 4: Can I Get a Rash with That?

I was about eight weeks pregnant when my endocrinologist and I decided it might be a good idea for me to get a continuous glucose monitor (CGM). I had considered getting one before, but similar to my hesitation about signing up for the insulin pump, I wasn't crazy about having yet another device attached to my body 24/7.

However, I was willing to do whatever was necessary and beneficial to ensure a healthy pregnancy and baby, so I went ahead and ordered a CGM. I honestly don't know what I would have done without it during my pregnancy. It was especially helpful when I went to the gym and when I slept because it alerted me if my blood sugar dropped too low.

However, one side effect that I was not anticipating was for my skin to break out in an itchy rash at the sensor site. I only wore the sensor for the suggested seven days before I switched sites and put on a new one, and I found that I usually started to itch where the sensor was by day two. By day four or five it was a real annoyance, and by the end of the week, I fantasized about the moment I got to rip that sucker off.

I told my doctor about my skin irritation from the adhesive, and she suggested that I spray some Nasacort on my skin prior to attaching the sensor in hopes of it acting as a barrier. I tried this and didn't see much of a difference. I just added it to my list of pregnancy annoyances and tried to forget about it.

But the rash battle waged on, and each one seemed to be worse than the last. I didn't think I could last until the end of my pregnancy enduring the itch, so I set out on a Google search to see if any fellow T1Ds had any other site suggestions that I could try in hopes that my rash problem was confined to my stomach. I also thought it would be good to find other site options since my belly was expanding. I learned that several people with CGMs prefer them on the back of their upper arm.

I must say, pulling off a CGM sensor and being able to get at the itch that I couldn't quite scratch was truly a satisfying feeling. I allowed myself a few minutes of scratch time before I slathered on some cortisone - ah, sweet relief.

I endured the adhesive rash for the entirety of my pregnancy. About a month postpartum, I decided to no longer wear the CGM since it was costing me $100 a month out of pocket and I really couldn't stand the thought of an eternal rash.

I went without a CGM for about two years until I decided I wanted to try for a second pregnancy. I started using the CGM again and was surprised that I no longer had a reaction to the adhesive like I did before. I wore a sensor for the entirety of my second pregnancy with no issue.

Chapter 5: I'm Feeling Pregnant

By 24 weeks pregnant, I was really starting to feel it. Heartburn, aches and pains, adjusting to my expanding midsection, dizziness, and insulin resistance – I had it all.

Let's start with the heartburn. I do not believe I ever experienced heartburn before pregnancy, certainly not enough for it to cause me any sort of discomfort or to recognize what it even was. That changed when I found myself pregnant, and I am now well aware of what heartburn feels like.

And then the aches and pains. I luckily escaped back pain and leg cramps, but I suffered from pelvic girdle pain for the majority of my pregnancy. In case you are wondering what that feels like, let me paint you a visual. It felt like I was doing some wild acrobatics on a balance beam made of granite when I slipped and racked myself right in the pubic bone.

It hurt to move my legs, to get dressed, to stand, sit, or lie down. Rolling over in bed was by far the worst – excruciating is a good term to use here. Unfortunately, like many other pregnancy symptoms, there wasn't much I could do for it. I just had to hope it went away after childbirth, which luckily it did. Ice packs and my amazing pregnancy body pillow were my best friends during this time.

I also experienced dizziness to the point where I almost started to black out. The first time it happened, I was at the gym just walking on the treadmill and when I stopped, I thought I was going to faint. I immediately thought my blood sugar had dropped low, but my sensor wasn't reading anything to confirm that.

The next time it happened, I was outside walking on a trail and started to feel lightheaded again, and it happened again one other time while walking at the gym. This was very frustrating, as I was committed to staying active during my pregnancy. From that point on, I decided to stick to riding the stationary bike, as I did not experience lightheadedness while doing that.

Now let's talk about insulin resistance. I had been waiting for the day, nervously dreading it, as I have read that by the end of pregnancy I could be taking three times as much insulin as I normally would.

By the middle of my second trimester, I noticed that my post-breakfast glucose was running higher than usual, even though I ate the same thing every day. Even after some correction boluses, it just didn't want to come down. My blood sugars weren't running scary high, but it was definitely higher than it had been in the previous weeks. With the help of my endocrinology team, we adjusted a few bolus rates and a basal rate, and things went back to normal.

Chapter 6: Birth Plans and Contemplation

Up until this point, I've shared lot of how I felt physically, so I thought I would share how I felt emotionally while pregnant.

As far as the childbirth process, I read the books, watched videos, talked to my friends, and witnessed the birth of my nephew, so I felt pretty confident about what to expect. Not every pregnancy is the same; therefore, not every labor and delivery is the same. I read a lot about birth plans – the mother's wish list of how she would like her labor and delivery to go. Birth plans are great, especially for those women who like to be in control (hi!).

Nevertheless, I made a birth plan and printed out a couple copies to bring to the hospital. As a second-time mom, I now laugh at my naivete. I included things like being able to walk around during labor, use of whirlpool during active labor, epidural when I asked for it, delayed cord clamping, skin-to-skin immediately after birth, and no pacifiers – all the things birth classes lead you to believe you want.

However, since my pregnancy was more complicated, I knew a birth plan for me would be more like a pipe dream. I came to the realization that my labor and delivery would most likely have unexpected turns, as I was told early on in my pregnancy that I may be induced during the 38th week to keep baby from getting too large, which is common among diabetic mothers. Since I knew that diabetic women are more likely to have larger babies, it also increased the risk of me having a C-section. Like a lot of women, I was hoping to have a vaginal delivery, but I realized that I may have to take another route.

The realization that I would not have a normal pregnancy and delivery is something I came to terms with years before I even got pregnant. I felt fortunate to have a healthy pregnancy that led to a healthy baby, and I put my trust in my doctors to decide what was best for me and my baby.

The only thing that I really wanted was having those crucial moments after delivery to cuddle and bond with my baby and attempt to breastfeed as soon as possible. That was the only part that concerned me about having a C-section. I knew that my time to bond with my child would be slightly delayed as I was sewed up and wheeled into recovery. Nonetheless, as long as everyone was healthy, that was the only thing that mattered.

As each day I felt more and more pregnant, it was certainly not lost on me that I would soon be a mother. I tried to imagine what life would be like once my baby was here, and what he would be like as he grew older. Like other expecting moms, I was both anxious and excited about my motherhood journey.

Chapter 7: My Favorite Thing

As I wrapped up the last week of my second trimester, I was getting more and more excited to meet my little guy, and I tried to embrace the better aspects of pregnancy.

My body was going through changes, and some areas were expanding that I wished wouldn't, but it was all part of the experience, resulting in the greatest gift. So instead of getting bummed out that my butt expanded with my belly, I tried to focus on the fact that it was because I would have a precious little boy in my arms in a few months.

Another added bonus of pregnancy is that if you're the first one back for a second helping of food, people think nothing of it, and they probably find it somewhat adorable. "Oh, that pregnant lady is back for more. How cute!" At least that's what I told myself.

With these hidden silver linings to pregnancy, my favorite thing had to be my belly. It's the most physical sign to yourself and the world that you have a little bundle of joy in there, and I couldn't help but find my hands constantly touching my stomach.

But there was more that I loved about my stomach than just its expanding shape – it was my physical link to my unborn son. Not only could I feel his kicks and tumbles on the inside, but when I laid my hands across my belly, I could feel him from the outside as well. He was quite the active little guy (some things never change!), and I got used to his patterns of activity.

My favorite time had to be first thing in the morning when I was lying in bed, just waking up. I would move a little as I woke up, and it was like my son sensed that it was morning because it wasn't long before I started to feel his kicks and movements. I never used to be much of a morning person, but every day I looked forward to this time, and I started to think of it as my favorite bonding time with my son.

Chapter 8: It's Complicated

At seven months pregnant, my HbA1c was 5.6%. All of my perinatal checkups were phenomenal. Baby was right on track with his growth and had no apparent birth defects – a "star baby," as my perinatologist called him.

With all of this great news, I couldn't help but feel extremely blessed. But even with an A+ report card, I was constantly brought back to reality when my doctor told me that starting at 32 weeks, I would be coming in for a scan every week because my risk for stillbirth was slightly higher since I'm diabetic; in his words, "In the later weeks of pregnancy, there is a higher risk for baby to die in utero." Gut blow.

While I liked my perinatologist a great deal, there was no denying the fact that he was a doctor and very matter of fact with the information he shared with me. I'm grateful for his brutal honesty, but it was difficult to hear my child could die in my womb because of my disease. He followed it up immediately that since my blood sugars had been so well controlled that my risk was very low, but he had already left a mark. The best I could do was to continue to monitor my blood sugars and eat well to keep my HbA1c as tight as I could.

I was further reminded of my unique situation when my husband and I began our baby class. I had been looking forward to this for a while. Of the eight couples in the room, I was the only one with type 1 diabetes, which wasn't a surprise.

Almost immediately I recognized my special circumstance of being a T1D expectant mother, as during our introductions the instructor had us share our biggest joy and challenge so far during pregnancy. While other mothers were sharing their struggles with anxiety over the delivery and being tired, which are legitimate pregnancy struggles, I shared having to monitor my blood sugars to ensure a healthy baby. And although I don't really consider it a challenge since I have done it for so long, it was something that I had to be hyper-aware of and think about 24/7, which the other women in the room did not.

I felt extremely blessed to even be pregnant and have such a healthy pregnancy, and the most important thing to me was having a healthy son and healthy delivery, but I couldn't help but feel a little left out on the options that typical mothers get to have.

My perinatologist told me that I would most likely be induced early, so I wouldn't even be able to go into labor on my own. I knew that the ultimate end goal was a healthy baby, and that is what I tried to focus on. It was hard for me to come to terms with the fact that I really didn't have much control over my labor and delivery. But really, who does?

One thing I knew I wanted to have control over while I was in labor was my diabetes management. I was hoping to wear my pump as long as possible and have my CGM on and check my own blood sugars. After being diabetic for 20 years, I know my body and I know my disease better than the nurses who would be charged with monitoring it.

At the end of the day, I know how lucky I was to be able to experience pregnancy, and I couldn't wait to be a mom to my son. I am blessed with an amazing husband whom I love dearly, and I knew he would be the greatest father. Looking forward to our new little family made the frustrations of being a pregnant diabetic completely worth it.

Chapter 9: The More You Know

I was a little disheartened about what I could expect when it came to labor and delivery being a type 1 diabetic, but I was determined to find information out there that reassured me that I could have an experience like any other expectant mother, so back to Google I went.

In my search, I ran across a blog of a woman sharing her experience as an expecting T1D, and she recommended the book *Balancing Pregnancy with Pre-Existing Diabetes: Healthy Mom, Healthy Baby* by Cheryl Alkon. Cheryl has lived with T1D for over 30 years, and she chronicled her experience with pregnancy on her blog, then ultimately wrote a book on the topic.

The book combined her experience with that of other T1D women and leading medical experts and the latest research on how to manage pregnancy with diabetes. I was ecstatic to learn of this. Published in 2010, it was current and didn't raise any red flags of diabetic pregnancy horror stories that abounded while doing internet research. I immediately hopped on over to Amazon and read the reviews and glanced inside the book. Liking what I was seeing, I ordered it right away.

It covers everything you need to know before getting pregnant, like getting your HbA1c down and stable, to what to expect on delivery day and postpartum. I really wished I would have found it earlier. While some of this information I already knew and some didn't apply to my current situation since I was almost three-fourths through my pregnancy, what I loved most about it was that it was relatable. It was written by a woman who experienced pregnancy with diabetes, and it had several accounts of different women's experiences as they managed their own diabetes through pregnancy.

I can't quite explain how much this book was profoundly reassuring to me and gave me the confidence that I was managing my diabetes to the best of my ability. It connected to me on a level that I just couldn't get from reading a general pregnancy book, or even information I got from my doctors. It weaved a thread that only other pregnant women with T1D can grasp.

The greatest thing I learned from it was that I had more control over my pregnancy and birth experience than I thought. There are women recounted in this book who took a stand and demanded not to be induced early unless medically necessary. If their HbA1c had been stellar and stable throughout their pregnancy, and the baby's growth was nothing out of the ordinary and there were no other health complications, they didn't see why they should have unnecessary medical interventions.

Of course, I wanted to ensure the health and safety of my child as well as myself, but if I had such tight control over my diabetes and no complications, why should I automatically be considered anything other than a healthy pregnant woman? I ultimately followed the advice of my medical team, but what I gained from this book was confidence in asking why something was being recommended for me and my pregnancy.

I learned that whatever my childbirth experience turned out to be, I knew that there were other women out there who could relate. And we have this unique, unseen bond. I highly recommend this book to any T1D woman planning to conceive.

Chapter 10: The Dawn Phenomenon

No, this is not a title for sci-fi novel. The "dawn phenomenon" is a real and often frustrating aspect of managing diabetes. The dawn phenomenon occurs in everyone, even those who are not diabetic, and is when the body produces extra glucose in the early morning hours (typically somewhere between 3:00 and 5:00 am) to ward off hypoglycemia during sleep. The phenomenon can continue to last after breakfast.

In a healthy person, their pancreas would produce insulin to counteract this extra glucose, thus keeping their blood sugar levels within a normal range. I've been aware of this phenomenon and have always had an early morning basal rate somewhat higher than the rest of the day to counteract the blood sugar spike.

In my third trimester, I noticed that this began to be amplified. I started noticing that my fasting blood sugars in the morning were hovering around the 110-130 range, which isn't terrible, but definitely not in the 80-90 range I preferred them to be.

I had also been struggling with my blood sugars continuing to rise after breakfast for about an hour or two, so I had to cut back the amount of carbs I ate in the morning to nearly half of what I was eating, and I increased my morning insulin-to-carb ratio. The rest of the day my blood sugars were on target and quite stable.

This was when my CGM came in handy. It was interesting to look at the graph and see my blood sugars trending along in the 70-90 range during the night (even after I treated a low blood sugar), and then like clockwork around 5:00 am, it started rising.

It was frustrating to say the least that I was doing everything right and yet my body reminded me who was really in charge.

Chapter 11: Week 32 and BPPs

Looking back, time flew by. I was fortunate that I had a relatively easy and healthy pregnancy. My blood pressure was fantastic, baby's heart rate was strong, and my regular Braxton-Hicks contractions were completely normal. My OB was happy with my weight gain and my blood sugars, so it seemed like everything was progressing right on target.

My OB did decide that since I am diabetic, she would induce me around 39 weeks, unless something changed. I was somewhat adamant against being induced, but I always knew it was going to be part of the plan for me. I came to terms with the fact that my delivery may not be what I hoped, but all that mattered was a healthy baby.

Along with controlling my food intake, I found that regular exercise helped control my weight gain and regulate my blood sugars. Exercise is important for anyone, especially pregnant women. For diabetic pregnant women, it is even more so. I really credit exercise for me having a healthy and smooth pregnancy.

Week 32 marked the beginning of my weekly appointments with my perinatologist for my baby's biophysical profile (BPP). From that point until I delivered, I went in for weekly scans to see how the baby was doing. The doctor checked the level of amniotic fluid, baby's movement, his practice breathing, and heart rate to make sure everything was okay.

At each appointment I got a score on an eight-point scale. A seven or an eight is great, but a six or below may require some more checking and could mean baby needs to come early. My doctor said as long as my blood sugars remained well controlled, the risk of something going wrong was very low. I left my first BPP appointment with an 8/8, so I was feeling confident that I could keep things under control until baby arrived.

Chapter 12: Week 33

It's funny how at one point in my pregnancy I was a little bummed about having to be induced early. By week 33, I was so anxious to meet my little guy that I was actually kind of looking forward to it. I talked to my doctor and knew what to expect from the induction, which helped me feel more comfortable with the process.

One thing I was excited about was that I was able to keep my insulin pump on and monitor my diabetes on my own. Knowing my body and being comfortable with my pump and CGM, this made me feel more at ease with my diabetes care during labor and delivery. This was huge. Most doctors and hospitals require diabetics to be hooked onto an insulin drip and completely monitor the mother's blood sugars according to their protocol. I was fortunate to have an endocrinologist who rallied for me and trusted me, and a hospital that was onboard with that plan.

One night as I lay in bed unable to sleep after getting up for a late-night trip to the bathroom, I couldn't help but think that our lives were about to be changed forever. It had been the two of us for nearly 10 years, and soon we would have this little person to be responsible for. We were very much excited and ready, but I knew it was going to be the biggest change of our lives. I thought about our son every day when I was pregnant, wondering what he would look like, what kind of person he would grow up to be. Even back then, I knew it was going to be the most amazing journey.

Chapter 13: Symphysis Pubis Dysfunction

During my 18th week of pregnancy, I began to feel pain in my pelvis. It literally happened overnight. I had gone for a three-mile walk the day before, and I thought that maybe I just overexerted myself a little and pulled a muscle. I had never experienced such pain before, but it felt like a strained groin.

However, days went by and the pain really wasn't going away. It hurt to walk, move my legs apart, and the worst was rolling over in bed or getting dressed. I wasn't due to see my OB for a few weeks, and it wasn't any pain that was extreme enough for me to give her a call. It was more of an annoyance and nothing I was really concerned about in regard to the pregnancy or health of the baby.

That led me to do some research of my own. So many people say to stay off the internet when it comes to researching medical symptoms, but I honestly found it quite comforting during my pregnancy to know that I shared a common experience with other women.

During my research into the extreme pain I was feeling in my pelvis, I ran across the term "symphysis pubis dysfunction," or SPD. During pregnancy, hormones are released that relax the ligaments and joints in a woman's body to prepare her for childbirth. Makes sense, right? However, sometimes they do too good of a job too early and can cause things to stretch too much. The symphysis pubis is the joint at the front of the pubic bone and if it becomes too loose it causes the pelvis to become misaligned, thus resulting in pain. Surprisingly, it's not something that many women have heard of in the U.S. To some degree, most pregnant women will experience some pain or ache in their pelvic region due to the growing fetus.

SPD is a bit more intense. I brought up my concern to my OB a couple of times, and she reassured me that what I was experiencing was normal. Unfortunately, from my reading, there wasn't much that could be done to relieve the pain. Once the baby is delivered, SPD typically goes away since hormones return to normal.

My experience with SPD was that it came and went. I had it for a few weeks fairly severely; I could barely walk when getting up in the morning, putting on pants was like torture, and rolling over in bed felt like someone was trying to rip my pelvis away from my body, but then it would subside a little.

Once I was in my 34th week, it was apparent that my baby was definitely growing and moving into the birthing position, and my SPD flared up big time. Even sitting normally caused the pain to radiate from my pubic bone. The best way to describe it is having someone repeatedly beat me in the pubic bone with a baseball bat. It was even tender to the touch.

The only thing that I found to help a little with the discomfort was to use ice packs a few times a day, and doing Kegel exercises seemed to strengthen the pelvic muscles and provide temporary relief. However, after a rough couple of days and thinking I had four and a half weeks to go, I broke down and bought a pelvic support belt that specifically targets the symphysis pubis. It did provide some relief, but SPD stuck with me through the end of my pregnancy.

The last trimester was no joke. Along with my very unfortunate pelvic pain, I also entered insulin resistance. My blood sugars remained under control and stable with adjustments to my pump, but it was just frustrating to see my numbers rise higher.

My morning blood sugars plagued me. I ran about 120-130 in the morning. One of my doctors suggested that I eat a little snack with protein before bed to combat this, but it didn't seem to work for me. I ended up cutting down what I ate in the morning to just a light Greek yogurt - a mere nine grams of carbs. This helped prevent my blood sugars from spiking out of control, but it still rose and took a while to come back down.

I tried keeping up with my exercise in hopes of maintaining stable blood sugars, but with my SPD, my options were guided by my comfort level. At that point, I was very ready to meet my son and regain some control of my body. With just a few weeks to go, I pushed through my pain and discomfort, and I continued to work hard to curb my blood sugar levels.

Chapter 14: Week 35

I swear, weeks seemed to fly by faster than ever. With only four weeks to go until my induction, I couldn't have been more ready or excited. I saw my endocrinologist for the last time before the birth during my 35th week. My HbA1c was 5.8%, and she said that since I was in such tight control of my blood sugars, there was no reason to see me again.

Looking back, I remember her telling me that she would like my HbA1c under 6.0% during my pregnancy and I thought it would be such a stretch to make that happen. Don't get me wrong, it was an incredible amount of work on my part to count all of my carbs and adjust my insulin needs accordingly, but I did it. It was possible. I honestly could not be prouder of myself for achieving something I could have only dreamed of. Obviously, my son is the best motivation I could have ever asked for when it came to managing my diabetes. I promised myself to continue to do so once he was born. However, I was looking forward to being able to eat something and not worry if my blood sugar decided to hang out in the high zone for a while.

My nesting instinct began to kick in around this time, so in my haste to do a deep clean of the kitchen one morning, I must have put a little too much strain on my back. Between that and the pelvic pain, I waddled around with the pace and gait of a fragile old lady. It was kind of nice to slow down for once.

Chapter 15: I Wish I Were Sleeping Right Now

By 36 weeks pregnant, to say that I was ready to have this baby is a gross understatement. We picked up the remaining baby items we needed, and I found myself more anxious than ever for our little guy to make his arrival.

Besides being beyond thrilled to meet my son, I was physically and mentally ready to push that little person out of me and regain a bit of myself. As I said from the beginning, I think I breezed through pregnancy relatively easily. I wasn't plagued with terrible nausea or vomiting, I continued to remain active throughout my pregnancy, and I successfully managed my diabetes through it all.

At my perinatal appointment during my 36th week, baby was estimated at weighing about 6 pounds, 13 ounces. I was really hoping this little guy would slide out around 7-7.5 pounds, but it looks like I was kidding myself. I estimated he was going to be at least an 8 pounder when he was born. Even though it seemed like he was tipping the scales before he was born, he was actually measuring in the 58th percentile, so only slightly above average. Everything else was looking good at that point – fluid was good, and he always passed his BPPs with flying colors.

My perinatologist asked me if I wanted to be induced during my 38th or 39th week, and although I was very anxious for this baby to come, I definitely wanted him to stay in there as long as he could to fully develop, so I chose the latter. Since my blood sugars had been so tightly controlled and there weren’t any complications, he was happy to accommodate me waiting until week 39 to induce.

Regarding my pregnancy symptoms at month nine: FATIGUE! I remember back in my first trimester battling a fatigue that I didn't know was possible, and it seemed to be back with a vengeance. I was literally tired all the time. Keeping my eyes open or my head from rolling back off my shoulders became an afternoon Olympic sport for me. At some point during the day, I would typically slide out of my chair and lay on the floor for several minutes.

Getting a full, uninterrupted night's sleep was non-existent for the majority of my pregnancy, so you'd think I would have gotten used to it. Nope.

One of the worst responses to a pregnant woman who says she is tired is to chuckle and say, "Well, you better get caught up on your sleep now, because you won't be getting any when the baby comes." I wanted to smack those people in the face.

Chapter 16: Let the Countdown Begin

The date was set. At my visit with my OB during my 37th week, the plan was made to get me into the hospital the night of August 30th to start my labor induction, with the baby hopefully arriving on the 31st.

Even though my blood sugars had been in such tight control and I didn't have high blood pressure or any complications, my perinatologist still preferred me to deliver this baby sooner rather than later, which wasn't a surprise. I seriously can't believe how fast that time went. But once I knew I was nearing the end of my pregnancy, the days started to drag by a little slower. It really became playing the waiting game and keeping myself occupied.

As far as my nerves went, I wasn't really nervous or scared about delivery at that point. I was just anxious to get in there and get this baby out. I didn't know what the pain of labor would be like, so I prepared myself for the worst and decided to get an epidural as soon as I couldn't handle it. I made peace with the idea that I may end up with a C-section. I trusted the doctors to make the best decision for me and my baby. All I kept focusing on was getting to hold my son for the first time and just marveling at this tiny person.

Chapter 17: Two Sleeps

Just days away from delivery day, time started to speed up again. At my last set of appointments, everything looked good. I was dilated about one centimeter, and my cervix was thinning out. I was hoping this would be favorable for my induction. I had wished he would come on his own before the induction, but with only two nights before I was due to the hospital, I started to doubt that he would make his grand entrance before then. All I knew is that I was ready, or at least I thought I was. I'm not sure if it hit me that in a few days I would be a mom and responsible for a tiny person, but I was ready for it.

Sleep had been fairly awful at that point, mostly because I became my own personal space heater. Heat radiated off me at all times. Being hot and sweaty at night was torture. Add in my horrible itchy stomach rash and I was pretty much miserable. I was very much looking forward to at least being a little more comfortable at night, even if I wasn't getting any sleep.

In the last few days before we headed to the hospital, I did my final cleaning of the house, making sure we were welcoming the baby to a clean home. After that, I tried to take it easy and relax as much as possible before delivery day.

Every day that passed, I got more and more excited to meet our son. I remember reading something that made me think of meeting my son for the first time and I just started crying. I knew it was going to be such an emotional moment meeting my son for the first time – just to see his face and touch him and hold him. I felt the love.

Overall, this pregnancy had been a good experience. I learned to go with the flow and take control over my health to ensure a healthy baby. Although every day wasn't always pleasant, I'd do it again in a heartbeat.

Chapter 18: The Big Day – Labor and Delivery

It still seems a surreal that the baby that was once rolling around in my tummy is now in my arms. Time seems to have flown by in the blink of an eye. A lot has happened in that amount of time.

My induction day finally rolled around, and it was a fairly normal start to the day. My husband and I got up and went about things as usual. We made a trip to the pet store so my husband could get the fish tank he had been wanting – good timing, right? My mom showed up at our house around 4:00 pm to stay and take care of the dogs while we were in the hospital.

It was about this time that it hit me that I was actually going to have a baby. I was a bit emotional, realizing the major event that was about to take place and how our lives would be changed forever. By the time we got to the hospital around 5:00 pm, I was feeling ready. We got checked into our room, which, to my husband's dismay, was windowless. It wasn't long before a nurse was in, inserting my IV and talking about what to expect.

The first order of business was for me to make sure that I could stay in charge of my diabetes and continue to wear my insulin pump. My doctor had ordered an insulin IV drip for me, but with the help of the nurse, we were able to convince her to allow me to continue to wear my pump until I went into active labor, and at that point we would reassess. This helped me feel a little more in control of the situation. I was also allowed to check my own blood sugars, and the nurses would just chart them every few hours. I am happy to say that throughout labor and delivery, my blood sugar never got above 100 or dipped below 70.

The first procedure to kick off my labor induction was to use a medication to soften the cervix. I had heard that this was a pill that was inserted next to the cervix, which is what I was expecting and received. The on-call doctor came in to check my cervix and insert the medication. Upon doing so, it was very uncomfortable and caused me to bleed quite a bit. His exact words were, "Not to alarm you, but there's quite a bit of blood." He then said there wasn’t anything wrong with me or the baby, and I just apparently had an angry cervix that didn't like being messed with.

Fifteen minutes after that fiasco, the nurse came in and told me she had made a mistake and read my doctor's orders wrong. My doctor had wanted me to take an oral medication that did the same thing as the cervical pills, so the on-call doctor would be coming back to fish them out. And so he returned, but he only managed to remove one of the two. At this point, I was a little frustrated with how my induction was going so far, and my fragile cervix didn't help matters.

It was now around 9:00 pm, and since I wasn't in active labor, I was allowed to order some food. Hallelujah! I wasn't very hungry, but figured it would probably be a while until I could eat again, so I ordered some soup, mashed potatoes, and fruit.

After dinner, we tried to get some rest. My husband had pulled the little couch mattress onto the floor and was able to sleep a little. I was in and out of it, especially with nurses coming in to check on me or fix the fetal monitor that kept coming loose every time I moved. At some point in the night I started to have contractions, but nothing terrible.

My doctor came in early the morning of delivery, and I was already on the Pitocin at that point. She checked my cervix and I had dilated some, which was good. The plan was to continue to increase the Pitocin every few hours to keep me progressing.

I was encouraged to get up and walk around, so my husband and I did several laps around the L&D floor, and we saw two other couples from our baby education class. It was nice to be able to get up and walk around, but the setting got very dull.

Later that morning, my doctor came back and decided to break my water, or at least she attempted to. After a few moments of her prodding around up there, her exact words were, "Wow, you must have a bag of steel!" Since she was unable to break my water, she decided to let me continue to progress and would try again later. I didn't even know this was possible. How could she not break my water?!

I continued to walk laps around the L&D floor. I eventually returned to my room, and my doctor came back and was finally able to successfully break my water. After that, labor continued to progress. My contractions weren't anything unbearable at that point, but I was getting tired.

Morning had turned into afternoon, and my labor was nearing 24 hours. I believe I was dilated about five centimeters and was quite exhausted when I decided to get an epidural. I really wanted to sleep but the contractions were keeping me from doing so. I was obviously delirious, believing I would get some sleep with an epidural. There would be no rest for me. The epidural went fine, but they started off giving me a very low dose, which didn't take the edge off my contractions like I had hoped.

Since I was unable to walk at that point, I began the epidural gymnastics, as I like to call them. My two nurses began a cycle of tossing me around into various positions every 30 minutes to keep my labor progressing. My personal favorite was being turned around on the bed onto my hands and knees, with a large bean bag tossed beneath me to lean on. Fortunately, all of my shame had been tossed by the wayside long before. I imagine it was quite a view.

It was around this time that my nurses made me aware that my little one wasn't loving my contractions. Every time I would have one, his heart rate would dip. Working with my doctor, the plan was to back off on the Pitocin and see how that went. That seemed to help with his heart rate, but that also meant my labor wouldn't progress as quickly. At this point they put oxygen on me and I really started to see where this was headed.

Eventually, my doctor came in and decided that it would be best to do a C-section. I was exhausted and nearly completely out of it at this point, and I was ready to do anything to get this baby out and be done with it. I always expected that I would end up with a C-section, so I was ready.

Once that was decided, it was like the room and everyone in it was put on fast forward. People were unhooking equipment, tossing papers at me, putting some sweet stockings and boots on my feet, a net on my head, and my husband was ushered into the bathroom and given scrubs. It seemed like only a matter of minutes before I was being wheeled off into the operating room. There was no emergency to my situation, they were only trying to get me in before another C-section would be needed.

I was wheeled into the operating room, which was bright and buzzing. There must have been at least a dozen people there, including the anesthesiologist that had administered my epidural only an hour or so earlier. He went to work upping my dose and making sure I was completely numb. Before I knew it, my OB was asking me if I could feel her stabbing me with a sharp instrument, and with my answer of "No," they were off to work.

It is the oddest feeling to be pain free but still feel the sensation of people cutting into you and tugging your body in ways that make you happy you can't feel pain. After what seemed like a matter of minutes, I could feel three sets of hands pushing on the top of my belly for what I can only imagine was to pop the baby out, and out he came!

I remember hearing him cry and everyone saying how big he was! And his chubby cheeks and hair! Before I could see him, I remember thinking, "How big is he?!" Then they popped him around the curtain and it was the most surreal feeling I've ever felt. Here was this baby, who was just inside of me, had been with me for nine months, and was now in front of my eyes. He was perfect in every way imaginable and he was finally here.

They quickly took him over to be weighed, measured, and warmed. My husband went over with him, and it was nice that I could still see them as the doctors sewed me up. I must admit that the anesthesia and whatever other drugs I was on had started to get to me and I was rather out of it, so I happily laid there on the table until they were ready to move me to the recovery room. That was the first time I got to hold my son. Another surreal moment. I kind of remember feeling like it was the most natural thing in the world to be holding my baby, yet at the same moment not really believing he was mine.

Once in the recovery room, we tried to breastfeed right away, but he was a little tired at first, so I just held him skin to skin until he was ready to try again. Breastfeeding and skin-to-skin contact were two of the most important things to me, so I was happy when it finally happened and he latched on.

While I was getting acquainted with our son, my husband was sent out to talk to our family; they were apparently bugging the staff about how things were going. I called that one, which is why I didn't want them at the hospital until after the baby was born, but I made an exception since I ended up having major surgery.

It wasn't long before I was sent upstairs, baby in my arms, to my postpartum room. At this point, I had been awake for 30-something hours and was medicated, so things get a little fuzzy. But after the nurses got me cleaned up and settled in, my husband and I were left with some alone time to bond with our new son. I think we were both in awe. After some bonding time, we allowed our family to come up and meet our son. There was a lot of love in that room that night, and it is one of my fondest memories of the experience.

That is my labor and delivery story. It certainly didn't go as planned, but, in truth, I never expected it to. Overall, it was a wonderful experience and I wouldn't change a thing. Though it was a long process, it brought me a healthy baby boy, and that's all I could ask for.

Post-birth, it's been quite the learning experience, and it makes my labor and delivery look like a cake walk. I will say that the first two weeks were the hardest, and it took a full month before I felt like I had a handle on things. Breastfeeding was probably the biggest struggle, getting things figured out and the engorgement and milk that was EVERYWHERE. Although it's been a complete life-changing event, I have loved becoming a mom and getting to know my son and watching him grow.

Chapter 19: My Little Time Accelerator

When we met with our pediatrician for the first time, I remember him saying that he likes to call babies "Time Accelerators," and boy is he right! The first 11 weeks of my son's life went by in a blink of an eye, marked by sleepless nights, diaper changes, and enough smiles and giggles to make my heart explode.

I remember at the start of my maternity leave not knowing how I would fill my day, but soon I wished for time to slow down without needing anything to occupy my time besides my son. I planned to return to work after 12 weeks of leave, and to say I wasn't ready to go back is an understatement. I never would have thought I would be someone who would consider being a stay at home mom, but given the opportunity, I would have done it in a heartbeat, at least for the first year or so.

My son and I were together every day since he was in my womb, and thinking of handing him over to daycare felt like someone would be cutting off a part of me. There was no way I was escaping that first day without major water works on my part. We developed such a strong bond, and I loved having him fill up my day with smiles and snuggles.

But, as my husband put it, going back to work was just what it meant to be a parent – at least for the majority of people in this country. Millions of women send their babies off to caregivers every day, and I would be no different. I knew it would get easier and both my son and I would get into a new routine, but it didn't make up for the fact that I would miss him.

This is what had been weighing most heavily on my mind. Just as we settled into a routine, we would be changing things up. Therefore, I tried to enjoy every minute of the remaining days of my leave and attempted to slow down time.

After the birth of my son, I felt like I was able to successfully handle getting my insulin levels and blood sugars under control. After the first few weeks of having quite a bit of lows due to breastfeeding and just no longer being pregnant, I was able to adjust my basal and bolus rates to where things stayed pretty stable.

My transition into motherhood was a learning experience, and though there have been difficult moments, they are fleeting, and what is left is a love that grows stronger by the day. This boy made me a mom and he's my whole world.

Chapter 20: Pregnancy, Take Two

I recently relived my experience as a pregnant type 1 diabetic, delivering another healthy baby boy in June 2018. It was much of the same in terms of managing my diabetes and seeing a perinatologist in addition to my OB. I elected for a repeat C-section, and since he was measuring on the larger side, he was delivered in my 38th week of gestation.

The pregnancy was very different this time, with me feeling worse physically. More nausea, more aches, more heartburn, and a more difficult delivery. But through all that, I am very grateful to have been blessed with another baby.

It wasn't until the birth of my second son that I realized how truly spontaneous the birth of a baby is. Do things ever goes as planned?

Just like my pregnancies, I had two very different births.

Because of my diabetes, my OB recommended to induce labor at 39 weeks with my first son. I expected this. I also expected my body not to cooperate. I just knew my baby boy wasn't ready to come out.

Sure enough, after 25 hours of labor and my son not responding well to contractions, the decision was made that it would be in his best interest to do a C-section. For some reason, I always knew this would be the way I would deliver my baby. So I wasn't panicked when it happened.

The surgery went smoothly, and within minutes I was listening to the first wails of my baby boy. A short time later, he was placed in my arms and we were wheeled off to recovery. It wasn't long until he was latched on to breastfeed and the pieces were falling into place as I hoped they would.

Fast forward a few years, and I was planning the birth of my second son. I opted for a repeat C-section because I didn't want to go through the process of a failed induction again. If I had spontaneously went into labor on my own before my surgery date, I would have rode it out, but I knew that wasn't likely to happen.

Since I had a previous C-section, I thought I knew what to prepare for. Boy, was I wrong.

There was no laboring, just prepping for surgery. As I walked into the OR and hopped on the table, I fully expected to be holding my newborn in a few minutes. But it would be hours before I would hold my sweet baby.

I knew things were starting to go off the rails when the doctors were having a difficult time popping my son's non-labored, round head through the incision. I felt like a rag doll as I was pressed and tugged. My doctor kept apologizing as minutes ticked by.

My excited anticipation of the arrival of my new baby had suddenly turned into a growing uncomfortableness. I just wanted it to be over.

My baby wasn't happy either. After trying to be forced through the surgical exit, he decided to try and make a run for it back up into my womb. He was finally delivered by my doctor grabbing his leg and pulling him out breech. He arrived 38 minutes after my surgery was scheduled to start.

It was immediately clear that something was off. Doctors and nurses picked up their pace and static noise elevated. I had yet to hear him cry.

While the doctors worked on sewing me up, my husband sat powerless by my side, watching a team of people rush into the room to get my son breathing. Unbeknownst to me, my son had officially "coded."

To this day, I do not know how long it was until his first breath, but it felt like hours.

Once they got him breathing and completed all the newborn checks, a nurse brought him over for me to see for the first time. The meeting was brief. Even though he was breathing on his own, he was whisked off to the NICU for observation.

Thanks to extreme nausea and vomiting post-surgery, it wasn't until later that evening that I felt well enough to make the trip down to the NICU to hold my son for the first time. He spent the first 24 hours of his life in the NICU, spending his first night on the outside away from me.

While I feel very fortunate that my son did only a brief stint in the NICU and I was able to bring a happy, healthy boy home after just two days, it was far from the outcome I had planned for.

I thought I knew what to expect going into the birth of my second child, but life proved once again that plans are meaningless.

Afterword

It's been over three years since I wrote those thoughts during pregnancy with my firstborn. I am so happy I chronicled my experience, as I've found the flurry of motherhood has swept a lot of those memories from my mind.

It is not lost on me how fortunate I have been to have had two healthy pregnancies and babies. There are definitely difficulties to carry a healthy baby while being a type 1 diabetic. It takes diligence.

My hope is that for any diabetic woman who reads this, know you are not alone. I've been there. I know your struggles, frustrations, and worries. I know the difficulties surrounding managing diabetes outside of pregnancy, let alone when you must consider the tiny person growing inside you. It's a lot to take on. But it's possible, and so tremendously worth it.

I continue to write about my experience as a mother through a realistic lens. Life with littles is loud, chaotic, and sleepless. I try to look at the lighter side of life and capture the humor that comes with parenthood. To read more about my life with a toddler and new baby, check out my blog, The Maternal Canvas, at thematernalcanvas.com.

Acknowledgements

Writing a book was always on my list of something I'd like to do, but I never thought it was tangible. I first must acknowledge all the teachers in my life who encouraged me to write, from my elementary teacher who laughed along with my silly poetry to my undergraduate and graduate advisors who told me I was a good writer while I plowed through my theses. Good teachers change lives, and I'm so fortunate to have met so many that made an impact.

I want to say thank you to the inspiring women in the writer's group of which I am so thankful to be a part. You ladies are what pushed me over the hump and encouraged me to get my words on the page.

I give credit to my friend, Jessi, for being my second set of eyes on this book. I can't think of a person better suited to go over my words with a fine-tooth comb. You are an expert of the English language and a true professional, and I am so grateful for your work.

Finally, I want to acknowledge my family for supporting me in sharing my story. I've come a long way from the shy, young girl who wanted to hide my disease because I longed to "fit in," to becoming a woman and mother who wants to share my story to reach other women to tell them they are not alone on their journey.

About the Author

Kendra is a mom to two beautiful boys, and partner to an incredibly patient husband. When not wrangling boys or writing words, she has a fond appreciation of art, yoga, and humor. You can read more about her take on life and motherhood on her blog, The Maternal Canvas.

Diagnosed with type 1 diabetes at the age of seven, Kendra has spent the majority of her life poking her fingers, counting carbs, and injecting insulin. She knows more about nutrition and the endocrine system than the average person, and despite having a faulty pancreas, she lives a happy and fulfilling life.

Made in the USA
Middletown, DE
14 October 2020